The Vegan KITCHEN

The Vegan KITCHEN

Feel-good food for happy and healthy eating

LOVE FOOD™

This edition published by Parragon Books Ltd in 2016
LOVE FOOD is an imprint of Parragon Books Ltd

Parragon Books Ltd
Chartist House
15–17 Trim Street
Bath BA1 1HA, UK
www.parragon.com/lovefood

ISBN: 978-1-4748-3791-0

Printed in China

Introduction and new recipes by Jane Hughes
Cover and new recipe photography by Tony Briscoe

NOTES FOR THE READER

This book uses both metric and imperial measurements. Follow the same units of measurement throughout; do not mix metric and imperial. All spoon measurements are level: teaspoons are assumed to be 5 ml, and tablespoons are assumed to be 15 ml. Unless otherwise stated, milk is assumed to be full fat, eggs and individual fruits and vegetables are medium, pepper is freshly ground black pepper and salt is table salt. A pinch of salt is calculated as 1/16 of a teaspoon. Unless otherwise stated, all root vegetables should be peeled prior to using.

The times given are an approximate guide only. Preparation times differ according to the techniques used by different people and the cooking times may also vary from those given.

Please note that any ingredients stated as being optional, are not included in the nutritional values provided. The nutritional values given are approximate and provided as a guideline only, they do not account for individual cooks, scales and portion sizes. The nutritional values provided are per serving or per item.

While the publisher of the book and the original author(s) of the recipes and other text have made all reasonable efforts to ensure that the information contained in this book is accurate and up to date at the time of publication, anyone reading this book should note the following important points: –
* Medical and pharmaceutical knowledge is constantly changing and the author(s) and the publisher cannot and do not guarantee the accuracy or appropriateness of the contents of this book;
* In any event, this book is not intended to be, and should not be relied upon, as a substitute for appropriate, tailored professional advice. Both the author(s) and the publisher strongly recommend that a doctor or other healthcare professional is consulted before embarking on major dietary changes;
* For the reasons set out above, and to the fullest extent permitted by law, the author(s) and publisher: (i) cannot and do not accept any legal duty of care or responsibility in relation to the accuracy or appropriateness of the contents of this book, even where expressed as 'advice' or using other words to this effect; and (ii) disclaim any liability, loss, damage or risk that may be claimed or incurred as a consequence – directly or indirectly – of the use and/or application of any of the contents of this book.
The publisher has been careful to select recipes that do not contain animal products. Any ready-made ingredients that could potentially contain animal products have been listed as 'vegan', so readers know to look for the vegan version. However, always read labels carefully and, if necessary, check with the manufacturer.

WHAT DOES IT MEAN TO BE A VEGAN?

Being vegan means not using any products that come from animals. It's not always just a dietary choice either, it is often also a lifestyle choice. Strict vegans avoid all animal products when choosing clothing, toiletries, medicine and cleaning products, as well as in their general diet.

People go vegan for many reasons, but the most common are:

~ Because they don't want to support practices that they believe are cruel to animals
~ Because they don't want to support practices that they believe are damaging to the environment
~ Because they believe that it would be easier to feed the world's population if more people were vegan
~ Because they believe that it is good for their health.

Of course, it's perfectly possible to be a 'junk food vegan', and to live on highly processed meat substitutes and vegan cupcakes piled high with colourful frosting! But most vegans respect their own health and many make other health-related changes to their diets by, for instance, avoiding alcohol, sugar or caffeine.

A well-balanced plant-based diet has many health benefits. You're likely to find yourself consuming less fat, especially less saturated fat and cholesterol. Fruits and vegetables are naturally high in fibre, and are good sources of vitamins A and C, whilst wholegrains and nuts are good sources of the B vitamins and vitamin E. Plant foods are also rich in antioxidants and phytochemicals which are believed to protect against some diseases, including certain cancers. Lots of vegans believe that a good, balanced vegan diet is very beneficial to their overall health.

In the following pages you'll find much more information about the steps you can take to make sure your vegan diet is good for you. You'll also find inspiring meal options that will prove you can eat exciting vegan-friendly food for any time of the day. Keeping your diet varied is key to enjoying a vegan lifestyle and this book provides lots of options for meals and snacks.

Divided into sections on breakfasts, lunches and snacks, mains, and desserts and baking, this book offers recipes for a variety of delicious dishes that everybody, including non-vegans, will enjoy. Vegetarians and meat-eaters will be surprised by how tasty some of these dishes are and so these meals are also good for entertaining a range of guests.

WHAT SHOULD YOU EAT TO BE A HEALTHY VEGAN?

The best way to maintain good health is to consume plenty of fresh fruit and vegetables, wholegrains, nuts, beans and pulses. These are key parts of a vegan diet so make sure to keep a good mixture in your day-to-day diet. Trying new foods and eating a variety of dishes will help to ensure that your body doesn't run low on anything it needs.

VITAMINS

There is only one important nutrient missing from a 100% plant-based diet, and that's vitamin B12, which only occurs naturally in animal-derived products. In the long term, a diet lacking in vitamin B12 can cause irreversible damage to the nervous system so it is important to monitor that you are taking on board enough of this vitamin.

The Vegan Society recommends that you take a B12 supplement and look for vegan foods that contain added vitamin B12, such as yeast extracts, nutritional yeast flakes, breakfast cereals and non-dairy milks.

Apart from vitamin B12, a diet based on fresh fruit and vegetables, pulses, nuts and wholegrains will provide a complete spectrum of vitamins. Good vegan sources of vitamin D include fortified margarines, non-dairy milks and breakfast cereals. It is essential to eat a good variety of food to make sure you are getting all your vitamins, rather than sticking to the same favourite meals.

MINERALS

A vegan diet includes a wide range of foods that are good sources of iron, including dark green leafy vegetables, beans and soya products. Consuming vitamin C at the same time helps our bodies to absorb iron – and many vegan foods contain iron and vitamin C together. It is also a good idea to drink a vitamin-C rich juice alongside a main meal to ensure that you consume vitamin C and iron together.

Iodine plays a part in thyroid regulation, and it's especially important if you're pregnant, as deficiency can harm your baby's brain development.

In the typical Western diet, the main source of iodine is milk – vegans obtain iodine from cereal products, sea salt and seaweeds like nori and kombu.

GOOD FATS

A vegan diet is naturally low in saturated fats and cholesterol. But we need to make sure that we still consume 'good fats' to get all the essential fatty acids that our bodies can't make on their own. Omega 6 is plentiful in a vegan diet, but unfortunately the most commonly recommended source of Omega 3 is fish oil.

The best vegan sources of Omega 3 are cold-pressed seed oils such as flaxseed, hemp seed and rapeseed oil, along with chia seeds, walnuts and Brazil nuts. These oils, seeds and nuts are available from most health food stores.

Vegan Omega 3 supplements are often made with marine algae. Some non-dairy milks are fortified with vegan-friendly Omega 3 oils. When buying any supplements, it is worth checking the packet to make sure that the oils are not provided in jelly-like capsules or lozenges that are made from the animal product gelatine.

CARBS AND FIBRE

Cutting out meat, dairy products and eggs has no negative effect on your consumption of fibre or carbohydrates – in fact a vegan diet is likely to contain more of these essential macronutrients as there is a lot of fibre in beans, pulses and fruit and vegetables. So as long as you ensure that you are eating a good range of these ingredients, your carbohydrate and fibre levels should be fine.

Wholegrain cereal products are a good choice for breakfast, not just because they contain more fibre than their white counterparts, but because the energy they contain is released gradually. This will give you more energy during the course of the day.

PROTEIN

Meat and eggs are called 'complete proteins' because they contain all the amino acids your body needs. Most plant foods don't contain all the essential amino acids – so you should aim to eat a variety of vegan protein sources including nuts, seeds, grains and pulses.

The notable exceptions are quinoa and soya – both of these plant foods are complete proteins. Tofu, in particular, is a food that is well worth investigating and although it can seem uninspiring when it's fresh from the pack, a little culinary know-how can transform it into a nutritious favourite. Marinating or braising tofu can perform wonders and turn this simple ingredient into something really tasty and versatile.

GOOD SUBSTITUTIONS

There are plenty of substitutions available in supermarkets and specialist health food stores for products that you may have eaten as a meat-eater or vegetarian. These can help keep away any cravings and provide more variety in your meals:

MEAT:
If you miss meat, experiment with substitutes such as vegan sausages and burgers, tofu, seitan and tempeh.

Hearty bean dishes and chunky mushrooms can also take the place of meat.

Quorn™ products are made with egg and so not suitable for vegans.

CHEESE:
Vegan cheeses are developing fast and there are many varieties available. You can also make vegan cheeses from scratch using ground nuts.

For sandwich fillings, try peanut and other nut butters, hummus and bean pâtés. Top jacket potatoes with spicy beans and curried vegetables.

Pizzas with roasted vegetables are just as good without cheese, and you won't notice the cheese is missing at all if you fold your home-made pizza into a calzone before baking it.

BUTTER:
Not all margarines are suitable for vegans – always check the label.

You can also spread savoury sandwiches with coconut oil, nut butters, hummus or mashed avocado.

MILK:
There are lots of non-dairy milks available, including sweetened and unsweetened, flavoured and organic varieties, based on soya, rice, oats, almonds, hemp seeds, coconuts, hazelnuts and more.

You can also make your own nut milks by blending your choice of nuts with water and then squeezing the liquid through a muslin bag. This milk can be used with cereals or to drink, as you would with cow's milk.

EGG:
There are several vegan egg substitutes available. These work well in baking and, depending on the recipe, you may also be able to substitute ground flax seeds or apple purée. The baking recipes in this book will suggest which product to use.

HONEY:
Agave nectar is a good alternative for honey and is suitable for use in cooking or for drizzling as you would do with honey.

You can also try maple or date syrup on porridge, and spreads made with dates and vegan chocolate or carob on toast.

FOODS TO CHECK

Vegan shoppers soon become used to reading the small print on food labels. As a short-cut, a quick look at the allergy advice on food labels should indicate whether they contain eggs or dairy products, as these are common allergens.

GELATINE:
Made from animal by-products, gelatine is used in a lot of low-fat foods, especially desserts and sweets, but also appears in margarines and breakfast cereals. It's also used to make the capsules for many health supplements.

LACTOSE:
This is a form of sugar derived from milk. Look out for it in gravy and stock powders, and in snacks such as potato crisps, where it is used as a flavour carrier.

SUGAR:
White sugar from sugar cane is sometimes whitened using a process that requires charcoal made with animal bones. White beet sugar is not subject to this process. If in doubt, choose brown sugar or try a substitute. Check any ready-made products that may contain sugar to ensure they are vegan-friendly.

COCHINEAL:
This red food colouring is made from crushed beetles.

QUORN™:
All Quorn™ currently contains egg.

WHEY:
This by-product of the cheese-making process is never vegan, and may not even be vegetarian if animal rennet has been used to separate the milk into curds and whey.

PASTRY:
This is often made with butter and sometimes made with lard. Glazed pastries are likely to have been brushed with milk or egg.

'FREE FROM':
Don't assume that any of the items on the 'Free From' shelf are vegan – they might be 'free from' dairy, or 'free from' eggs, but not both. Gluten-free products often rely on eggs to hold them together.

WAX:
Several kinds of wax can be used to enhance the shine and shelf-life of fruit and vegetables. Some waxes are made from paraffin or petroleum, but others may contain non-vegan animal-based products such as shellac. At present, most food labelling doesn't give these details. Look for produce that is seasonal and grown locally, as this is less likely to have had wax added as a preservative to help it travel long distances. There are vegetable washing products available, but if in doubt, ask the store's Customer Services and Technical Department and peel your purchases.

HOW TO STOCK YOUR FOOD CUPBOARD

Knowing how to stock a vegan-friendly food cupboard is a great way to keep organized in the kitchen. Locating a good wholefood shop in your area can be a revelation, but you can always find everything you need online. Most supermarkets are also now getting better at stocking vegan-friendly foods, with lots of ordinary supermarkets now stocking a range of non-dairy milks and margarines.

Make smart purchases by selecting products such as soya milks, breakfast cereals and snack bars that contain added nutrients. Make sure your larder includes foods that are fortified with vitamin B12, such as yeast extracts and nutritional yeast flakes.

Try to stock a selection of nuts, seeds, grains and beans so that your protein intake varies from day to day. Do not buy nuts and seeds in bulk unless you can store them in the fridge, as their high fat content means that they can deteriorate quickly. Tinned beans are always useful and will save you a lot of soaking and cooking time.

As you modify your way of eating, you may decide to experiment with juicing and sprouting seeds and grains. Sprouting can be done in a jam jar covered with muslin, but if you become a juicing enthusiast you may want to invest in a macerating juicer, which will extract juice from leafy green vegetables and wheatgrass.

Raw food is another branch of veganism worth investigating. Many raw dishes can be made without unusual ingredients or equipment, but a well-stocked wholefood store should provide specialist ingredients to help you develop your repertoire. A powerful blender is a good investment.

It's important to allow for sweet treats and savoury snacks so that you don't feel as if you are missing out. Dark chocolate is a vegan mainstay, and crunchy nuts and seeds toasted with spices can be useful when travelling. There are lots of recipes for vegan snacks in this book so these will help to stave off hunger when you are out and about.

Vegan sandwiches or lunches can be hard to find when you're out in the main high street shops or in cafés, so it's worth carrying some snacks or a vegan cereal bar or two in your bag in case you don't find anywhere vegan-friendly to eat.

BREAKFASTS

SPICED QUINOA BREAKFAST BOWL WITH PECAN NUTS

Quinoa is packed with protein, making it a fantastic grain to include in a healthy breakfast. Here it's combined with zingy spices, sweet pears and crunchy nuts for a breakfast that's worth getting out of bed for.

SERVES: 2
PREP: 15 MINS COOK: 15 MINS

55 g/2 oz uncooked quinoa, rinsed well
150 ml/5 fl oz water
1/4 tsp ground cinnamon
1/4 tsp ground nutmeg
1/4 tsp ground allspice
pinch of salt
4 tsp maple syrup
125 ml/4 fl oz almond milk
1 pear, cored and diced
35 g/1 1/4 oz toasted pecan nuts

1. In a small saucepan, combine the quinoa with the water, cinnamon, nutmeg, allspice and salt and bring to the boil over a medium-high heat. Reduce the heat to low, cover and simmer for about 15 minutes, until the quinoa is tender.

2. Stir in the maple syrup and divide the mixture between two serving bowls. Pour the almond milk over the top, dividing equally, and top with the pear pieces and pecan nuts. Serve immediately.

KEEN ON QUINOA?

Quinoa is native to Peru and Bolivia where it was known as 'the golden grain' of the Incas. It is said to be the only plant food that contains all nine essential amino acids, putting it on par with animal protein.

PER SERVING: 320 KCALS | 15.5G FAT | 1.4G SAT FAT | 42.9G CARBS | 17.3G SUGARS | 6.8G FIBRE | 6.1G PROTEIN | 0.8G SALT

MILLET PORRIDGE WITH APRICOT PURÉE

Gluten-free millet makes a good replacement for oats and the apricots will boost your iron intake for the day.

SERVES: 4
PREP: 5 MINS COOK: 25 MINS

225 g/8 oz millet flakes
450 ml/15 fl oz soya milk
pinch of salt
freshly grated nutmeg, to serve

APRICOT PURÉE
115 g/4 oz dried apricots, roughly chopped
300 ml/10 fl oz water

1. To make the apricot purée, put the apricots into a saucepan and cover with the water. Bring to the boil, then reduce the heat and simmer, half covered, for 20 minutes until the apricots are very tender. Use a hand-held blender or transfer the apricots, along with any water left in the saucepan, to a food processor or blender and process until smooth. Set aside.

2. To make the porridge, put the millet flakes into a saucepan and add the milk and salt. Bring to the boil, then reduce the heat and simmer for 5 minutes, stirring frequently, until cooked and creamy.

3. To serve, spoon the porridge into four bowls and top with the apricot purée and grated nutmeg.

BOOST THE FLAVOUR

Use plump, soft apricots to give a smooth purée. Sprinkle a little nutmeg over the top for extra flavour, if preferred.

PER SERVING: 289 KCALS | 3G FAT | 1G SAT FAT | 52G CARBS | 12G SUGARS | 2.5G FIBRE | 4.5G PROTEIN | 0.6G SALT

SUNSHINE SALAD WITH MUESLI COOKIES

This sunny bowl of colourful citrus fruits combined with delicious muesli cookies is a great way to start the day.

MAKES: 2 SALADS AND 30 COOKIES
PREP: 25-30 MINS
COOK: 15 MINS, PLUS COOLING

FRUIT SALAD

1 large orange
1 grapefruit
1 ruby grapefruit
2 tsp maple syrup

COOKIES

160 g/5¾ oz vegan margarine
300 g/10½ oz brown sugar
175 g/6 oz plain flour
½ tsp baking powder
40 g/1½ oz linseed meal (ground golden linseeds)
1 tsp ground cinnamon
½ tsp salt
125 ml/4 fl oz soya milk
1 tsp vanilla extract
50 g/1¾ oz raisins
50 g/1¾ oz dates, finely chopped
50 g /1¾ oz walnuts, finely chopped
250 g/9 oz porridge oats

1. Preheat the oven to 180° C/350° F/Gas Mark 4. Line a large baking sheet with baking paper.

2. To make the cookies, cream together the margarine and sugar in a large mixing bowl until light and fluffy. Sift together the flour and baking powder and stir into the bowl with the linseed meal, cinnamon and salt.

3. Whisk together the soya milk and vanilla extract in a small bowl and stir into the mixture, adding the raisins, dates, walnuts and oats at the same time. Mix until thoroughly combined.

4. Roll a little of the cookie mixture into a ball about 4 cm/1½ inches in diameter. Place on the prepared baking sheet and flatten slightly. Continue with the rest of the mixture to make about 30 small cookies. Bake in the preheated oven for 15 minutes, or until golden. Leave to cool on the sheet for 5 minutes before transferring to a wire rack to cool completely.

5. To make the salad, use a sharp knife to peel away all the skin and pith from the orange and grapefruits. Carefully cut v-shaped wedges between each segment of the fruit to remove the flesh without the membranes. Divide the fruit between two small serving dishes and drizzle with maple syrup to taste. Serve each fruit salad with two cookies (remaining cookies should be stored in a container and consumed within 5 days).

PER SERVING: 482 KCALS | 13.6G FAT | 1.6G SAT FAT | 88.7G CARBS | 54.4G SUGARS | 9.2G FIBRE | 7.5G PROTEIN | 0.4G SALT

HERBY TOFU SCRAMBLE

Vegan ciabatta topped with delicious tofu and cherry tomatoes makes a healthy and filling breakfast or lazy weekend brunch that's hard to beat.

SERVES: 2
PREP: 15 MINS COOK: 15 MINS

400 g/14 oz firm tofu
12 cherry tomatoes on the vine
1 tbsp olive oil, for roasting
1 small vegan ciabatta loaf
25 g/1 oz vegan margarine
2 garlic cloves, halved and bruised
5 tbsp chopped fresh mixed herbs, (tarragon, chives, parsley)
1 tsp smoked paprika
salt and pepper (optional)

1. Preheat the oven to 200° C/400° F/Gas Mark 6. If the tofu is packed in water, drain it and press the tofu block between sheets of kitchen paper to remove as much water as possible. Gently crumble the tofu into a large bowl.

2. Place the cherry tomatoes in a medium-sized roasting tin and drizzle lightly with olive oil. Roast in the preheated oven for 5 minutes, or until warm and beginning to split.

3. Cut the ciabatta loaf in half and slice each half lengthways. Toast the bread slices lightly on both sides.

4. Melt the margarine in a large frying pan over a medium heat. Sauté the garlic in the margarine for 1 minute, then remove the garlic from the pan and discard.

5. Put the tofu into the frying pan over a medium heat and fry it in the garlic-infused oil, turning occasionally, for 3–4 minutes, or until just browning. Remove from the heat, stir in the chopped fresh herbs, and add salt and pepper to taste, if using.

6. Sprinkle the tofu scramble with smoked paprika. Serve the scramble immediately on the toasted ciabatta, with the roasted tomatoes on the side.

PER SERVING: 738 KCALS | 38.1G FAT | 5.6G SAT FAT | 64.7G CARBS | 3.8G SUGARS | 9.2G FIBRE | 41.9G PROTEIN | 1.8G SALT

MUSHROOMS ON BRUSCHETTA

Nutritious mushrooms are star of this simple topped vegan baguette. It can be cooked in a flash and is best enjoyed warm.

SERVES: 4
PREP: 15 MINS COOK: 10 MINS

12 slices vegan baguette, each 1 cm/½ inch thick
3 tbsp olive oil
2 garlic cloves, crushed
225 g/8 oz chestnut mushrooms, sliced
225 g/8 oz mixed wild mushrooms
2 tsp lemon juice
2 tbsp chopped fresh flat-leaf parsley
salt and pepper (optional)

1. Place the slices of baguette on a ridged griddle pan and toast on both sides until golden. Reserve and keep warm.

2. Meanwhile, heat the oil in a frying pan. Add the garlic and cook gently for a few seconds, then add the chestnut mushrooms. Cook, stirring constantly, over a high heat for 3 minutes. Add the wild mushrooms and cook for a further 2 minutes. Stir in the lemon juice.

3. Season to taste with salt and pepper, if using, and stir in the chopped parsley.

4. Spoon the mushroom mixture onto the warm toast and serve immediately.

MIGHTY MUSHROOMS

The compounds in mushrooms, which help boost the immune system, help to prevent cancers, infections and auto-immune diseases.

PER SERVING: 327 KCALS | 12.3G FAT | 1.8G SAT FAT | 45.1G CARBS | 4.9G SUGARS | 3.6G FIBRE | 11.3G PROTEIN | 1.1G SALT

SPINACH AND SWEET POTATO PANCAKES

Savoury pancakes are a great alternative to sweet, especially when they are filled with healthy baby spinach and crunchy pine nuts.

SERVES: 4
PREP: 20 MINS COOK: 30 MINS

200 ml/7 fl oz soya milk
50 g/1¾ oz plain flour
50 g/1¾ oz chickpea (gram) flour
100 g/3½ oz sweet potato, grated
1 small red onion, finely chopped
2 tbsp vegetable oil, for frying

FILLING

150 g/5½ oz fresh baby spinach leaves, shredded
20 g/¾ oz currants
1 tbsp olive oil
25 g/1 oz pine nuts
salt and pepper (optional)

1. To make the filling, place the spinach in a saucepan over a medium heat. Add a splash of water and cook for about 2–3 minutes or until wilted. Turn out onto a plate, then blot firmly with kitchen paper to squeeze out as much water as possible. Set aside.

2. To make the pancakes, whisk together the soya milk, plain flour and chickpea flour in a large bowl. Stir in the sweet potato and onion, and mix thoroughly.

3. Heat the vegetable oil in a large frying pan over a high heat and pour a quarter of the pancake mixture into the pan, using the back of a spoon to spread the mixture out to the edges of the pan. Fry for 2–3 minutes on each side, turning carefully, until brown and crisp. Transfer to a plate lined with kitchen paper and keep warm. Make three more pancakes.

4. Return the spinach to the saucepan with the currants, olive oil and pine nuts and place over a medium heat. Season with salt and pepper, if using, and cook for a minute or until heated through. Take a quarter of the spinach mixture and place on one half of a pancake. Fold over the other half. Repeat with the remaining pancakes.

STACK 'EM UP

Use the pancake mixture to make 8–10 mini pancakes and serve as stacks, alternating pancakes with the filling.

PER SERVING: 307 KCALS | 16.4G FAT | 1.5G SAT FAT | 33.1G CARBS | 9.2G SUGARS | 4.6G FIBRE | 8.5G PROTEIN | 0.2G SALT

HOME-MADE CACAO AND HAZELNUT BUTTER

This healthy hazelnut butter is delicious for breakfast, plus it keeps well for several days.

MAKES: 225 G/8 OZ
PREP: 15 MINS, PLUS STANDING COOK: 3-4 MINS

115 g/4 oz unblanched hazelnuts
25 g/1 oz raw cacao powder
70 g/2½ oz light muscovado sugar
125 ml/4 fl oz light olive oil
½ tsp vanilla extract
pinch of salt

1. Add the hazelnuts to a dry frying pan and cook over a medium heat for 3–4 minutes, constantly shaking the pan, until the nuts are an even golden brown in colour.

2. Wrap the nuts in a clean tea towel and rub the outsides to remove the skins.

3. Put the nuts into a blender and blend until finely ground. Add the cacao powder, sugar, oil, vanilla extract and salt, and blend again to make a smooth paste.

4. Spoon into a small preserving jar and clip the lid in place. Leave to stand at room temperature for 4 hours, until the sugar has dissolved completely. Stir again, then store in the refrigerator for up to 5 days.

SUITS YOU

This can be served many ways but it is really delicious spread on tasty vegan wholegrain toast.

PER 45G SERVING: 430 KCALS | 40G FAT | 5.2G SAT FAT | 19.5G CARBS | 13.9G SUGARS | 4G FIBRE | 4.1G PROTEIN | 0.3G SALT

CHEWY APRICOT AND ALMOND ENERGY BARS

These flapjack-style, vegan energy bars are great for carrying with you for a healthy mid-morning snack.

MAKES: 15
PREP: 25 MINS, PLUS COOLING COOK: 30 MINS

115 ml/3¾ fl oz coconut oil
85 g/3 oz light muscovado sugar
60 g/2¼ oz almond butter
1 dessert apple, cored and coarsely grated
150 g/5½ oz porridge oats
40 g/1½ oz brown rice flour
55 g/2 oz unblanched almonds, roughly chopped
40 g/1½ oz sunflower seeds
200 g/7 oz dried apricots, diced

1. Preheat the oven to 180°C/350°F/Gas Mark 4. Line a 20-cm/8-inch shallow square cake tin with non-stick baking paper.

2. Heat the oil and sugar in a medium-sized saucepan over a low heat until the oil has melted and the sugar is dissolved. Remove from the heat and add the almond butter, stirring until melted.

3. Add the apple, oats, flour, almonds and sunflower seeds and mix well together.

4. Spoon two thirds of the mixture into the prepared tin and firmly press down. Sprinkle over the apricots and firmly press into the base layer, then dot the remaining oat mixture over the top in a thin layer so that some of the apricots are still visible.

5. Bake in the preheated oven for about 25 minutes, until the top is golden brown. Remove from the oven and leave to cool in the tin until almost cold, then cut into 15 small rectangles. Leave to cool completely, then lift the bars out of the tin, using the paper. Separate the bars and pack into a plastic container. Store in the refrigerator for up to 3 days.

PER BAR: 235 KCALS | 14G FAT | 7.2G SAT FAT | 26.6G CARBS | 14.6G SUGARS | 3.5G FIBRE | 4.2G PROTEIN | TRACE SALT

BANANA FLATBREAD BITES WITH TAHINI AND DATE SYRUP

Sometimes the best things are the simplest. Assembled in minutes, this speedy breakfast is perfect for a busy morning.

SERVES: 4

PREP: 15 MINS COOK: 5-6 MINS

4 x 20-cm/8-inch vegan wholemeal tortillas
4 tbsp tahini
3 tbsp date syrup
4 bananas, peeled

1. Preheat a dry frying pan, then add the tortillas, one by one, and warm for 30 seconds each side.

2. Arrange the tortillas on a chopping board, thinly spread each with the tahini, then drizzle with the date syrup. Add a whole banana to each tortilla, just a little off centre, then roll up tightly.

3. Cut each tortilla into thick slices, secure the bites with a cocktail stick and arrange on a plate. Serve warm.

GO BANANAS

Bananas are the only fruit to contain both tryptophan and vitamin B6, which produce serotonin – the natural chemical that helps lift your mood.

PER SERVING: 354 KCALS | 11.3G FAT | 2.5G SAT FAT | 60G CARBS | 25.4G SUGARS | 4.1G FIBRE | 9.4G PROTEIN | 0.5G SALT

RAW DATE AND COCONUT BARS

These chunky, nutty bars get the most out of power-packed raw ingredients. Perfect to keep you energized at work all morning long.

MAKES: 12
PREP: 30 MINS, PLUS CHILLING   COOK: NONE

400 g/14 oz medjool dates, halved and stoned
60 g/2¼ oz unblanched almonds
60 g/2¼ oz cashew nut pieces
35 g/1¼ oz chia seeds
2 tbsp maca (powdered superfood)
2 tsp vanilla extract
20 g/¾ oz desiccated coconut
55 g/2 oz unblanched hazelnuts, very roughly chopped
25 g/1 oz pecan nuts, broken in half

1. Put the dates, almonds and cashew pieces in a food processor and process until finely chopped.

2. Add the chia seeds, maca and vanilla extract and process again until the mixture binds together in a rough ball.

3. Tear off two sheets of non-stick baking paper, put one on the work surface and sprinkle with half the coconut. Put the date ball on top then press into a rough rectangle with your fingertips. Cover with the second sheet of paper and roll out to a 30 x 20-cm/12 x 8-inch rectangle. Lift off the top piece of paper, sprinkle with the remaining coconut, the hazelnuts and pecan nuts, then re-cover with the paper and briefly roll with a rolling pin to press the nuts into the date mixture.

4. Loosen the top paper, then transfer the date mixture, still on the base paper, to a tray and chill for 3 hours or overnight, until firm.

5. Remove the top paper, cut the date mixture into 12 pieces, peel off the base paper then pack the bars into a plastic container, layering with pieces of baking paper to keep them separate. Store in the refrigerator for up to 3 days.

PER BAR: 225 KCALS | 11G FAT | 2G SAT FAT | 31.7G CARBS | 23.5G SUGARS | 5.4G FIBRE | 4.2G PROTEIN | TRACE SALT

VEGETABLE STOMACH-SOOTHING JUICE

To keep your tummy in tip-top health, choose this appealing vegetable stomach soother, which is enriched with a little hemp seed oil that adds an important boost of polyunsaturated fat and vitamin E.

SERVES: 1
PREP: 20 MINS COOK: NONE

3 oranges, zest and a little pith removed
1 carrot, halved
2 tomatoes, roughly chopped
125 ml/4 fl oz chilled water
1 small green chilli, halved
2 celery sticks, thickly sliced
2 tsp hemp seed oil

1. Cut two oranges in half and feed them and the carrot through a juicer. Pour the juice into a blender.

2. Roughly chop and deseed the remaining orange, then place it, the tomatoes and water into the blender and whizz until smooth.

3. Add the chilli and celery and whizz again until blended. Pour the juice into a glass, stir in the hemp seed oil and serve immediately.

GO FOR ORANGE

Vitamin C, the antioxidant vitamin that boosts the immune system and protects from the signs of ageing, is found in abundance in oranges.

PER SERVING: 302 KCALS | 10.5G FAT | 1.4G SAT FAT | 50.3G CARBS | 37.1G SUGARS | 8G FIBRE | 5.8G PROTEIN | 0.1G SALT

KIWI QUENCHER

A combination to get you glowing from the inside out: jewel-like kiwi fruit blended with juicy green grapes and thirst-quenching lettuce.

SERVES: 1
PREP: 15 MINS COOK: NONE

- ½ romaine lettuce
- 4 kiwi fruit, peeled
- 115 g/4 oz green grapes
- 1 large pear, halved
- handful of ice, to serve (optional)

1. Peel off a lettuce leaf and reserve. Feed the kiwi fruit and grapes, lettuce and pear through a juicer.
2. Half-fill a glass with ice, if using, then pour in the juice.
3. Decorate with the reserved lettuce leaf and serve immediately.

SUPER KIWI

A single kiwi contains more immune-boosting vitamin C than the recommended daily allowance and as much potassium as a small banana.

PER SERVING: 431 KCALS | 2.8G FAT | 0.3G SAT FAT | 106G CARBS | 68G SUGARS | 5G FIBRE | 8.5G PROTEIN | 0.1G SALT

RAW COCOA MILKSHAKE

Great for waking up your taste buds first thing, or for a nutritious chocolate hit any time, this delicious milkshake provides the perfect pick-me-up.

SERVES: 4
PREP: 10 MINS COOK: NONE

400 ml/14 fl oz almond milk
85 g/3 oz dried dates
85 g/3 oz cashew nuts
2 tbsp vegan raw cocoa powder
1 tsp ground cinnamon
handful of ice cubes
1 tbsp orange zest, to decorate

1. Place the almond milk, dates, cashew nuts, cocoa powder, cinnamon and ice into a blender.

2. Blend thoroughly until the milkshake is a thick pouring consistency.

3. Pour into chilled glasses, decorate with the orange zest and serve immediately.

CHOOSE CASHEWS

A daily dose of cashews could help improve your memory and protect against age-related memory loss.

PER SERVING: 198 KCALS | 10.8G FAT | 2G SAT FAT | 24.9G CARBS | 15.5 SUGARS | 3.9G FIBRE | 5.2G PROTEIN | 0.1G SALT

LUNCHES AND SNACKS

SMASHED AVOCADO AND QUINOA WRAP

Brimming with nourishing, natural goodness, fresh avocado and spinach combine with colourful, crunchy raw red cabbage to create these really appealing quinoa-topped wraps. Great for sharing as everyone can assemble their own.

SERVES: 4

PREP: 20 MINS, PLUS COOLING   COOK: 15-18 MINS

175 g/6 oz quinoa
400 ml/14 fl oz vegan stock
1 large, ripe avocado, peeled and stoned
½ tsp smoked paprika
2 garlic cloves, crushed
grated zest and juice of 1 lemon
4 vegan wholemeal tortillas
50 g/1¾ oz baby spinach
150 g/5½ oz red cabbage, finely sliced
salt and pepper (optional)

1. Place the quinoa and vegan stock in a small saucepan and simmer, covered, for 15–18 minutes, or until the stock has been fully absorbed. Set aside to cool.

2. Meanwhile gently mash the avocado flesh with the smoked paprika, crushed garlic, lemon zest and just enough lemon juice to make a thick consistency.

3. Spread the mashed avocado down the centre of each wrap and then top with the warm quinoa, spinach and red cabbage. Season with salt and pepper, if using. Tuck in the ends and tightly fold or roll into a wrap and serve immediately.

RED CABBAGE FOR HEALTH

Red cabbage is rich in compounds that help to protect us from cancers and the signs of ageing It is also higher in vitamin C than pale varieties and is a good source of minerals, including calcium and selenium.

PER SERVING: 385 KCALS | 13.2G FAT | 2.8G SAT FAT | 56.8G CARBS | 3.6G SUGARS | 10.4G FIBRE | 11.8G PROTEIN | 1.4G SALT

KEEN GREEN SOUP

This soothing soup will cool you down on a hot day. It is easy to make and is perfect for a summer lunch that is packed with goodness.

SERVES: 2
PREP: 10-15 MINS COOK: NONE

180 g/6¼ oz cucumber
2 celery sticks
2 tbsp chopped fresh parsley
2 tbsp chopped fresh mint
2 tbsp chopped fresh coriander
250 ml/9 fl oz chilled water
2 fresh parsley sprigs, to garnish

1. Chop the cucumber and celery and add to a blender with the parsley, mint, coriander and water. Blend until smooth.

2. Serve immediately or chill in the refrigerator and stir just before serving, garnish with a sprig of parsley.

TAKE A FRESH LOOK AT PARSLEY

You may think parsley is just a herb for garnishes, but think again as this mighty green is packed full of important nutrients and you don't need to use much to enjoy the benefits of it. Parsley is rich in calcium and potassium and has lots of iron and phosphorus. Just 2 tablespoons of parsley contain a whopping 153 per cent of the recommended daily allowance of vitamin K (which works with protein to help strengthen bones).

PER SERVING: 26 KCALS | 0.2G FAT | TRACE SAT FAT | 5.1G CARBS | 2.3G SUGARS | 1.9G FIBRE | 1.3G PROTEIN | 0.1G SALT

WARM QUINOA, ROAST PUMPKIN AND PINE NUT SALAD

Quinoa has long been prized for its flavour and ability to keep you feeling full. Loaded with protein and vitamins, it is perfect for a salad.

SERVES: 2
PREP: 20 MINS   COOK: 30 MINS

100 g/3½ oz white quinoa, rinsed
350 ml/12 fl oz cold water
200 g/7 oz pumpkin flesh, cut into bite-sized chunks
3 tbsp olive oil
¼ tsp cayenne pepper
20 g/¾ oz pine nuts
25 g/1 oz fresh flat-leaf parsley, roughly chopped
20 g/¾ oz baby spinach
juice of ¼ lemon
salt and pepper (optional)
2 lemon wedges, to serve

1. Preheat the oven to 180°C/350°F/Gas Mark 4. Put the quinoa in a saucepan. Add the water, bring to the boil, then cover and simmer over a very low heat for 10 minutes. Remove from the heat, but leave the pan covered for a further 7 minutes to allow the grains to swell. Fluff up with a fork.

2. Meanwhile, put the pumpkin and 2 tablespoons of oil in a large roasting tin, sprinkle with the cayenne and a pinch of salt, if using, and toss well. Roast for 25 minutes, or until crisp on the edges and tender. Tip into a large bowl.

3. Toast the pine nuts in a dry frying pan over a high heat until they are light brown, then tip them into the bowl. Gently mix in the quinoa, parsley and spinach, taking care that nothing breaks up, then season with salt and pepper, if using.

4. Divide the salad between two plates, drizzle with the remaining oil and the lemon juice, and serve with lemon wedges for squeezing over.

PERFECTLY COOKED

Cooked quinoa should have a texture similar to slightly chewy couscous, but be careful not to overcook it. If the pan boils dry during cooking, add a splash more water and turn off the heat, then leave for 10 minutes with the lid on; the trapped steam should be enough to finish cooking the quinoa without saturating it.

PER SERVING: 521 KCALS | 37G FAT | 4.5G SAT FAT | 40.5G CARBS | 2.0G SUGARS | 4.6G FIBRE | 9.9G PROTEIN | 1.5G SALT

BARLEY AND CRUSHED BEAN SALAD

Tossed with summery vegetables, pearl barley makes a filling salad. It's packed with complex carbs and soluble fibre and is a low-GI food.

SERVES: 4

PREP: 10-15 MINS COOK: 25-30 MINS

1.2 litres/2 pints vegan stock
150 g/5½ oz pearl barley
425 g/15 oz broad beans, podded (175 g/6 oz podded weight)
150 g/5½ oz peas
2 spring onions, quartered
2 stems of fresh tarragon, finely chopped
25 g/1 oz fresh flat-leaf parsley, finely chopped
25 g/1 oz pea shoots

DRESSING

2 tbsp flaxseed (linseed) oil
2 tbsp rice bran oil
1 tbsp vegan white wine vinegar
1 tsp vegan Dijon mustard
1 tsp coriander seeds, roughly crushed
¼ tsp crushed dried red chillies
pepper (optional)

1. Put the stock in the base of a steamer, bring to the boil, then add the pearl barley, cover and simmer for 20 minutes. Put the broad beans in the top of the steamer, then put it on the steamer base, cover and steam for 5–10 minutes, or until the barley and beans are just tender.

2. Drain off the stock and discard, then spoon the barley into a salad bowl. Add one third of the broad beans and raw peas. Put the remaining broad beans and peas, the spring onions, tarragon and parsley in a food processor and process until finely chopped. Add to the salad bowl.

3. To make the dressing, put the flaxseed oil, rice bran oil, vinegar, mustard, coriander seeds and chillies in a jam jar, season with pepper, if using, screw on the lid and shake well. Drizzle over the salad and toss gently together, then spoon into four bowls, top with the pea shoots and serve.

PROTEIN BOOSTERS

Proteins are an essential constituent of virtually every cell in the body; in fact the word comes from the Greek meaning 'of prime importance'. They are needed for growth and repair of body tissues, to make up enzymes and hormones and as neurotransmitters. Unlike meat, most vegetable proteins do not contain all nine essential amino acids, so aim to mix different vegetable proteins together in one meal by serving grains and pulses together.

PER SERVING: 265 KCALS | 15.7G FAT | 3.3G SAT FAT | 22.7G CARBS | 3.6G SUGARS | 5.9G FIBRE | 7G PROTEIN | 2.9G SALT

OAT TABBOULEH

We tend to think of oats as being just for porridge or flapjacks, but if you buy wholegrain oats, often called 'oat groats', they make a delicious, nutty-tasting salad base that is packed with energy-boosting complex carbs and fibre.

SERVES: 4

PREP: 10-15 MINS COOK: 30-35 MINS

- 1.2 litres/2 pints vegan stock
- 175 g/6 oz oat groats
- 4 spring onions
- 300 g/10½ oz asparagus
- 1 courgette, diagonally sliced
- 25 g/1 oz fresh mint, roughly chopped

DRESSING

- grated rind and juice of 1 lemon
- 1 tbsp hemp oil
- 3 tbsp olive oil
- 1 tsp cumin seeds, finely crushed
- 1 tsp coriander seeds, finely crushed
- pepper (optional)

1. Pour the stock into a saucepan, bring to the boil, then add the oats. Simmer for 25 minutes, or until the oats are tender and the grains have split. Drain off the stock through a sieve and discard, then spoon the oats into a salad bowl and leave to cool.

2. To make the dressing, put the lemon rind and juice, hemp oil, olive oil, cumin seeds and coriander seeds in a jam jar, season with a little pepper, if using, screw on the lid and shake well.

3. Preheat a griddle pan over a high heat. Put the onions, asparagus and courgette in a bowl, drizzle over half the dressing and toss together. Cook in the hot pan for 2–3 minutes, or until just softened and beginning to char, turning from time to time. Leave to cool, then transfer to a clean chopping board and cut into bite-sized pieces.

4. Add the remaining dressing to the oats and stir. Add the cooled vegetables, sprinkle with the mint and toss gently together. Spoon into four shallow bowls to serve.

AMAZING ASPARAGUS

In traditional folk medicine, asparagus was used as a tonic and sedative. We know it best for its antioxidant properties; it is rich in beta carotenes and B group vitamins, plus vitamins C and E. It is not suitable for those who suffer with gout, as it is one of the few vegetables high in purines.

PER SERVING: 348 KCALS | 18.2G FAT | 3.2G SAT FAT | 37G CARBS | 4.4G SUGARS | 7.4G FIBRE | 10.2G PROTEIN | 2.8G SALT

KALE AND GREEN GARLIC BRUSCHETTA

Green or 'wet' garlic is the garlic from the very first crop of the season. Soft and delicious, it is excellent spread on wholegrain toast.

SERVES: 4

PREP: 25 MINS COOK: 25 MINS

1 green garlic bulb
3 tbsp olive oil
4 slices vegan bread, total weight 250 g/9 oz
85 g/3 oz shredded kale, rinsed well and drained
1 tbsp balsamic vinegar
2 tsp pomegranate molasses
salt and pepper (optional)

1. Preheat the oven to 190° C/375° F/Gas Mark 5. Put the garlic bulb on a piece of foil, drizzle with 1 tablespoon of the oil, then wrap the foil around it and seal well. Put on a baking sheet and roast in the preheated oven for 20 minutes, or until the bulb feels soft when squeezed.

2. Meanwhile, preheat a ridged griddle pan. Cut the bread slices in half, brush one side of each with a little oil, then cook the bread, oiled-side down, in the hot pan for 2 minutes. Brush the top with the remaining oil, then turn and cook the second side until golden brown.

3. Unwrap the garlic, peel away the outer casing from the bulb, separate the cloves, then remove any of the tougher skins. Crush the creamy soft garlic to a coarse paste using a pestle and mortar. Mix the paste with any juices from the foil, then thinly spread on the griddled bread and keep warm.

4. Heat a dry, non-stick frying pan, add the kale and cook over a medium heat for 2–3 minutes, until just wilted. Mix in the vinegar, molasses and a little salt and pepper, if using. Arrange the bruschetta on a chopping board, spoon over the kale and serve.

GO GREEN

Green, leafy vegetables like kale, chard and cabbage are rich in iron and contain the pigment chlorophyll, which helps to increase the oxygenation of blood cells.

PER SERVING: 278 KCALS | 12.7G FAT | 1.7G SAT FAT | 35.4G CARBS | 3.6G SUGARS | 4.8G FIBRE | 7.3G PROTEIN | 1.4G SALT

SPICY PEANUT SOUP

This spicy and satisfying soup gets rich flavour from peanut butter and a kick from herbs and chillies. Serve it with hunks of crusty bread for dunking or over steamed rice.

SERVES: 4

PREP: 15 MINS COOK: 35-40 MINS

1 tbsp vegetable oil
1 small onion, chopped
1 tbsp finely chopped fresh ginger
2 garlic cloves, finely chopped
1/2 tsp ground cumin
1/4 tsp pepper
1/4 tsp ground cinnamon
1/4 tsp cayenne pepper
1/4 tsp turmeric
1 1/2 tsp salt
3 serrano chillies, finely chopped
350 g/12 oz sweet potatoes, peeled and diced
750 ml/1 1/4 pints vegan stock
400 g/14 oz canned chopped tomatoes, with their can juices
125 g/4 1/2 oz unsweetened peanut butter
125 ml/4 fl oz coconut milk
juice of 1 lemon
2 tbsp chopped fresh coriander leaves
2 spring onions, thinly sliced, and chopped fresh coriander sprigs, to garnish (optional)

1. Heat the oil in a medium-sized saucepan over a medium heat. Add the onion and cook, stirring frequently, for 10 minutes until soft. Stir in the ginger, garlic, cumin, pepper, cinnamon, cayenne pepper, turmeric and salt.

2. Add the chillies, sweet potatoes and stock and increase the heat to medium-high. Bring the mixture to the boil, then reduce the heat to medium-low and simmer for 20 minutes until the sweet potatoes are tender.

3. Add the tomatoes with their can juices and the peanut butter. Purée the soup in a blender. Return the soup to the pan and stir in the coconut milk, lemon juice and coriander. Heat over a medium heat until heated through. Serve hot, garnished with the spring onions and coriander sprigs, if using.

GO NUTS

Peanuts are a great source of copper, an essential mineral for red blood cell formation and for building a healthy immune system, blood vessels and bones.

PER SERVING: 402 KCALS | 26.6G FAT | 9.2G SAT FAT | 34.9G CARBS | 13.3G SUGARS | 5.8G FIBRE | 11.7G PROTEIN | 4.5G SALT

GRILLED VEGETABLE FILO TARTS

These perfectly-formed parcels are filled with delicious grilled vegetables – perfect for a light lunch or starter.

SERVES: 6

PREP: 30 MINS, PLUS COOLING COOK: 20 MINS

1 tbsp olive oil, for brushing
4 large sheets of vegan filo pastry
pinch of salt
1 small aubergine, sliced into 2-cm/3/4-inch rounds
18 cherry tomatoes
1 large red pepper, halved and deseeded
1 tbsp capers
6 Kalamata olives, pitted and sliced
12 basil leaves, shredded
salt and pepper (optional)

1. Preheat the oven to 160° C/325° F/Gas Mark 3. Lightly oil six fluted metal tartlet tins.

2. Cut the filo pastry into 24 x 13-cm/5-inch squares. Cover with a clean damp cloth. Lightly brush 4 squares with oil. Sprinkle with a tiny pinch of salt.

3. Stack the squares on top of each other, rotating so that the corners are offset like the petals of a flower.

4. Place the stack in a tartlet tin, pressing well into the edge. Repeat with the remaining squares.

5. Bake in the preheated oven for 7–8 minutes, until golden. Remove from the oven and keep warm. Preheat the grill to high.

6. Place the aubergine, tomatoes, and the red pepper cut-side down, on a roasting tray. Lightly brush the aubergine slices with oil. Place under the preheated grill for 10–12 minutes, or until the red pepper and tomatoes are slightly blackened and the aubergine is golden.

7. Cut the aubergine into bite-sized chunks. Remove the skin from the pepper. Cut the flesh into small squares.

8. Carefully remove the pastry cases from the tins and fill with the vegetables. Lightly season with salt and pepper, if using. Scatter over the capers, olives and basil and serve warm.

WHY NOT TRY?

This is really easy to adapt depending on what ingredients you have to hand. Try adding mushrooms or onions to the filling and top with chilli for a spicy kick.

PER SERVING: 138 KCALS | 3.7G FAT | 0.5G SAT FAT | 23.3G CARBS | 5.2G SUGARS | 4.1G FIBRE | 3.7G PROTEIN | 0.4G SALT

PLAIN CHOCOLATE AND PEANUT BUTTER ENERGY BALLS

Vegan-friendly chocolate containing more than 80 per cent cocoa is one of the star ingredients of the healthy kitchen if used in small amounts.

MAKES: 8

PREP: 15 MINS, PLUS CHILLING COOK: NONE

50 g/1¾ oz almond flour
60 g/2¼ oz unsweetened peanut butter
20 g/¾ oz unsalted peanuts, roughly chopped
3 tbsp linseeds
25 g/1 oz vegan chocolate with 85% cocoa, finely chopped
1 tsp vegan cocoa powder
salt (optional)

1. Put the almond flour in a food processor and process for a minute, until you have the texture of rough flour.

2. Put the peanut butter, peanuts, flaxseeds, chocolate and a small pinch of salt, if using, in a bowl and mix. Add the almond flour, reserving 1½ tablespoons. Mix until you have a texture resembling chunky clay.

3. Sprinkle the remaining almond flour and the cocoa powder onto a plate and mix with a teaspoon. Form a tablespoon-sized blob of the peanut mixture into a ball using your palms. Roll it in the cocoa powder mixture, then transfer to a plate. Make a further seven balls in the same way.

4. Cover and chill in the refrigerator for at least 30 minutes, or up to two days.

ALSO TRY THIS

If the coating of cocoa powder is too bitter and strong for your taste, substitute it with a teaspoon of ground cinnamon.

PER BALL: 144 KCALS | 11.9G FAT | 2.1G SAT FAT | 5.9G CARBS | 1.7G SUGARS | 3G FIBRE | 4.9G PROTEIN | 0.3G SALT

APPLE AND CINNAMON CRISPS

Crisp and crunchy, without the fat, salt and strong flavours of potato crisps, these make a much healthier alternative for all the family.

SERVES: 4

PREP: 20-25 MINS, PLUS COOLING COOK: 1½–2 HOURS

1 litre/1¾ pints water
1 tbsp salt
3 dessert apples, such as Braeburn or Gala
¼ tsp ground cinnamon

1. Preheat the oven to 110°C/225°F/Gas Mark ¼. Put the water and salt into a large mixing bowl and stir until the salt has dissolved.

2. Very thinly slice the apples, one at a time, with a sharp knife or mandolin, leaving the skin on and the core still in place, but removing any pips. Add each apple slice to the water. Turn to coat in the salt water, which will help prevent discoloration.

3. Drain the apple slices in a colander, then lightly pat dry with a clean tea towel. Arrange in a thin layer on a large cooking or roasting rack. Place this in the oven so that the heat can circulate under the slices as well as over the tops.

4. Bake for 1½–2 hours, until the apple slices are dry and crisp. Loosen with a palette knife and transfer to a large plate or chopping board, then sprinkle with cinnamon. Leave to cool completely, then serve.

KEEP COOL

Pack any leftovers into a plastic container, seal and keep in the refrigerator for up to 2 days.

PER SERVING: 72 KCALS | 0.2G FAT | TRACE SAT FAT | 19.1G CARBS | 14.2G SUGARS | 3.4G FIBRE | 0.3G PROTEIN | 0.7G SALT

BEETROOT HUMMUS

This brightly-coloured hummus combines chickpeas and deep-pink beetroot to make this fantastically vibrant dip. Serve with vegetable crudités for dipping.

SERVES: 4
PREP: 15 MINS COOK: NONE

400 g/14 oz canned chickpeas, drained and rinsed
1 garlic clove, roughly chopped
100 g/3½ oz cooked beetroot
1½ tbsp tahini
juice of ½ lemon
3 tbsp olive oil
salt and pepper (optional)

1. Place the chickpeas, garlic and beetroot in a food processor or blender and process until broken into crumbs.

2. Add the tahini and lemon juice and process again, pouring in the olive oil until the hummus is the consistency you like. Season to taste with salt and pepper, if using.

3. Serve the hummus with vegetable crudités.

DID YOU KNOW?

The dark-green purple-tinged leaves of the beetroot are an edible vegetable, too, and can be sliced and steamed. Like the root, they are rich in vitamins, minerals and carotenes.

PER SERVING: 212 KCALS | 14.3G FAT | 1.9G SAT FAT | 15G CARBS | 5.1G SUGARS | 4.8G FIBRE | 5.3G PROTEIN | 0.1G SALT

ROSEMARY, SEA SALT AND SESAME POPCORN

Forget about fat-and additive-laden potato chips – popcorn can be cooked in a fraction of the oil for a healthier alternative.

SERVES: 4
PREP: 10-15 MINS COOK: 6-8 MINS

40 g/1½ oz sesame seeds
2 tbsp olive oil
2 rosemary stems, torn into large pieces
200 g/7 oz popping corn
1 tsp sea salt
2 tbsp balsamic vinegar

1. Add the sesame seeds to a large frying pan with 1 teaspoon of the oil. Cover and cook over a medium heat for 2–3 minutes, shaking the pan from time to time, until the seeds are toasted golden brown and beginning to pop. Scoop out of the pan into a bowl and wipe out the pan with a piece of kitchen paper.

2. Add the remaining oil and the rosemary to the pan and heat gently, shaking the pan to release the rosemary's oil. Add the corn, cover with the lid and cook over a medium heat for 3–4 minutes, shaking the pan, until all the popcorn has popped.

3. Remove from the heat and sprinkle with the toasted sesame seeds and season with the salt and vinegar, then tip into a serving bowl, discarding the rosemary just before eating.

GET POPPING

Popcorn is a natural wholegrain and a great source of complex carbohydrates. Stay away from the buttery and sugary toppings as these are less healthy.

PER SERVING: 304 KCALS | 13.7G FAT | 1.9G SAT FAT | 39.7G CARBS | 1.2G SUGARS | 9.2G FIBRE | 6.8G PROTEIN | 1.5G SALT

FIVE-SPICE CASHEWS

Chinese five spice is a popular seasoning mixture in Chinese cooking. Made up of equal parts Szechuan peppercorns, star anise, fennel seeds, cloves and cinnamon, it is both sweet and spicy.

SERVES: 8

PREP: 5 MINS, PLUS COOLING   COOK: 10-12 MINS

1 tbsp groundnut oil, for oiling
1/2 tsp Szechuan peppercorns
2 star anise pods
1/2 tsp fennel seeds
6 whole cloves
1/2 tsp ground cinnamon
2 tbsp water
50 g/1 3/4 oz soft light brown sugar
1 tsp salt
250 g/9 oz unsalted toasted cashew nuts

1. Preheat the oven to 200° C/400° F/Gas Mark 6. Lightly oil a baking tray and a large piece of foil.

2. In a spice grinder, grind together the peppercorns, star anise pods, fennel seeds and cloves until finely ground. Add the cinnamon and mix well.

3. Put the water and sugar into a medium-sized saucepan and heat over a medium heat, stirring constantly, for 2 minutes, or until the sugar is dissolved. Add the spice mixture and salt and stir to mix well. Add the nuts and stir to coat completely. Cook, stirring, for a further minute.

4. Transfer the nuts to the prepared baking tray and spread out in an even layer. Roast in the preheated oven for 6–8 minutes until most of the liquid has evaporated. Transfer the nuts to the prepared foil and separate them so that they don't stick together. Leave to cool completely before serving.

5. Store in an airtight container at room temperature for up to 2 weeks.

DID YOU KNOW?

Many supermarkets carry Chinese five spice. Look for it in the spice section and substitute 2 1/2 tsp of the mix for the Szechuan peppercorns, star anise, fennel seeds, cloves and cinnamon.

PER SERVING: 219 KCALS | 16.2G FAT | 3.2G SAT FAT | 16.6G CARBS | 7.6G SUGARS | 1.1G FIBRE | 4.8G PROTEIN | 0.8G SALT

MAINS

ROAST VEGETABLE PIZZA

You might think that pizza is off the vegan menu but think again! This version is just as delicious, with colourful roast vegetables and home-made tomato sauce.

MAKES: 2 PIZZAS PREP: 30 MINS, PLUS COOLING AND RISING COOK: 50 MINS

1 tbsp olive oil, for greasing
1 green pepper, deseeded and sliced
1 red or yellow pepper, deseeded and sliced
1 courgette, sliced
1/2 small aubergine, sliced
1 red onion, sliced
3 tbsp olive oil
1 onion, finely chopped
2 garlic cloves, crushed
400 g/14 oz canned chopped tomatoes
1 tsp brown sugar
1 tsp sun-dried tomato purée
1 tsp dried oregano
10 g/1/4 oz fresh basil leaves, torn
6 black olives, halved
1 tbsp pine nuts

PIZZA BASE

375 g/13 oz strong white flour
1 tsp salt
1 tbsp caster sugar
7 g /1/4 oz easy-blend dried yeast
2 tbsp olive oil
10 g/1/4 oz strong white flour, for dusting

1. Preheat the oven to 200° C/400° F/Gas Mark 6. Lightly grease two baking sheets. Put the peppers, courgette, aubergine and red onion into a large bowl with 2 tbsp of olive oil and mix well until coated with oil. Transfer to a roasting tin and roast for 30 minutes, or until just starting to brown. Remove from the oven and set aside.

2. To make the sauce, heat 1 tbsp of oil in a large frying pan. Fry the onion for 4–5 minutes, then add the garlic and cook for a further minute. Stir in the tomatoes, sugar, purée and oregano. Simmer gently for 6–8 minutes, until very thick. Remove from the heat and leave to cool.

3. To make the pizza base, sift together the flour, the salt, the sugar and yeast in a large bowl. Stir in the oil and 225 ml/8 fl oz of warm water. Turn the mixture out onto a floured surface and knead for 8–10 minutes. Roll into 2 x 25-cm/10-inch rounds and place on the two prepared sheets. Mix the basil into the sauce and spread evenly over the bases. Top with the olives, vegetables and pine nuts. Leave to rise in a warm place for 20 minutes. Increase the oven to 230° C/450° F/Gas Mark 8. Bake for 10–12 minutes, or until golden brown. Leave to cool for 5 minutes then serve.

PER PIZZA: 1316 KCALS | 49.6G FAT | 6.6G SAT FAT | 186.4G CARBS | 32.5G SUGARS | 15.2G FIBRE | 32.6G PROTEIN | 3.2G SALT

SPICY STUFFED PEPPERS

These rice-stuffed peppers are great for a dinner party as they look really impressive but are actually easy to make.

SERVES: 4

PREP: 25 MINS, PLUS SOAKING COOK: 40-45 MINS

4 red peppers
3 sprays of olive oil spray
1 onion, finely chopped
2 garlic cloves, chopped
2.5-cm/1-inch piece fresh ginger, peeled and grated
1 fresh serrano chilli, deseeded and chopped
1 tsp ground cumin
1 tsp ground coriander
85 g/3 oz cooked brown basmati rice
1 large carrot, about 115 g/ 4 oz, grated
1 large courgette, about 85 g/3 oz, grated
25 g/1 oz ready-to-eat dried apricots, finely chopped
1 tbsp chopped fresh coriander
pepper (optional)
150 ml/5 fl oz water
fresh herbs, to garnish

1. Preheat the oven to 190° C/375° F/Gas Mark 5. Cut the tops off the peppers and reserve. Discard the seeds from each pepper. Place the peppers in a large bowl and cover with boiling water. Leave to soak for 10 minutes then drain and reserve.

2. Place a large frying pan over a medium heat and spray with the oil. Add the onion, garlic, ginger and chillies and fry for 3 minutes, stirring frequently. Sprinkle in the ground spices and continue to cook for a further 2 minutes.

3. Remove the pan from the heat and stir in the rice, carrot, courgette, apricots, chopped coriander and pepper to taste, if using. Stir well, then use to stuff the peppers.

4. Place the stuffed peppers in an ovenproof dish large enough to allow the peppers to stand upright. Put the reserved tops in position. Pour the water around their bases, cover loosely with the lid or foil and bake in the preheated oven for 25–30 minutes, or until piping hot. Serve garnished with herbs.

WHY NOT TRY

If you like your dishes extra spicy, add another fresh serrano chilli.

PER SERVING: 120 KCALS | 1.4G FAT | 0.1G SAT FAT | 25G CARBS | 12.7G SUGARS | 5.5G FIBRE | 3.6G PROTEIN | TRACE SALT

RED CURRY WITH MIXED LEAVES

This dish does it all – it's ideal for a quick mid-week meal but is impressive enough to serve for family and friends as well.

SERVES: 4
PREP: 15 MINS COOK: 20 MINS

2 tbsp groundnut oil
2 onions, thinly sliced
1 bunch of fine asparagus spears
400 ml/14 fl oz coconut milk
2 tbsp vegan red curry paste
3 fresh kaffir lime leaves
225 g/8 oz baby spinach leaves
2 small heads of pak choi, chopped
1 head of Chinese leaves, shredded
10 g/¼ oz fresh coriander, chopped

1. Heat a wok over a medium-high heat and add the oil. Add the onions and asparagus and stir-fry for 1–2 minutes.

2. Add the coconut milk, curry paste and lime leaves and bring to the boil over a low heat, stirring occasionally.

3. Add the spinach, bok choi and Chinese leaves and cook, stirring, for 2–3 minutes, until wilted. Add the coriander and stir well. Serve immediately.

WHY NOT TRY

You can serve this dish straight from the wok without any sides, but if you prefer to have an accompaniment it is delicious served with freshly cooked rice.

PER SERVING: 367 KCALS | 29.3G FAT | 20.2G SAT FAT | 18.2G CARBS | 8G SUGARS | 6.4G FIBRE | 8.6G PROTEIN | 0.6G SALT

WHOLE BAKED CAULIFLOWER

Low-fat, cholesterol-free and loaded with vitamin C, cauliflower is baked whole and served with a tasty tomato, olive and caper sauce. Fibre and protein-packed butter beans add to the mix in this warming supper dish.

SERVES: 4
PREP: 20-25 MINS COOK: 1 HOUR

1 tbsp olive oil
2 onions, finely sliced
4 garlic cloves, chopped
2 tbsp vegan red wine vinegar
pinch of soft brown sugar
70 g/2½ oz black olives, stoned
2 tbsp capers
3 tbsp roughly chopped fresh basil
800 g/1 lb 12 oz canned chopped tomatoes
400 g/14 oz canned butter beans, drained and rinsed
150 ml/5 fl oz vegan stock
1 large cauliflower, leaves trimmed
salt and pepper (optional)
2 tbsp basil sprigs, to garnish

1. Heat the olive oil in a saucepan that is large enough to fit the whole cauliflower in.

2. Add the onions and garlic and fry, over a medium heat, until soft and translucent. Stir in the vinegar, brown sugar, black olives, capers and basil and heat through for a further 2–3 minutes. Pour in the tomatoes, butter beans and vegan stock. Stir well and bring the sauce to a simmer for 5–6 minutes, stirring occasionally.

3. Sit the cauliflower head upside down on a chopping board and, using a sharp knife, carefully cut the tough stem away. Place the cauliflower into the centre of the tomato sauce, pushing it down so half is covered by the sauce. Season with salt and pepper, if using.

4. Reduce the heat to low, cover and simmer for approximately 45 minutes, or until the cauliflower is tender. Carefully stir once or twice during cooking to prevent the sauce catching on the base of the pan. Serve immediately, garnished with basil.

HEAT IT UP

To reheat this dish if you have made it in advance, simply transfer to a roasting dish, drizzle with olive oil and place in a warm oven until hot.

PER SERVING: 242 KCALS | 7.3G FAT | 1G SAT FAT | 34.6G CARBS | 14.2G SUGARS | 11.5G FIBRE | 1.1G PROTEIN | 9.6G SALT

SPICY AUBERGINE AND CHICKPEA CASSEROLE

This hearty Middle Eastern-style vegan stew is packed with rich, spicy flavours and is full of healthy vegetables.

SERVES: 6

PREP: 25 MINS COOK: 55 MINS

- 4 tbsp olive oil
- 1 large onion, chopped
- 1 tbsp cumin seeds, crushed
- ½ tsp allspice berries, crushed
- ½ tsp salt
- ¼ tsp pepper
- 2 garlic cloves, thinly sliced
- 1 large red pepper, deseeded and cut into 2.5-cm/1-inch pieces
- 2 aubergines, thickly sliced and cut into segments
- 800 g/1 lb 12 oz canned chickpeas, drained and rinsed
- 400 g/14 oz canned chopped tomatoes
- 500 ml/17 fl oz vegan stock
- ½ head of cabbage, about 280 g/10 oz, tough stems removed
- salt and pepper (optional)
- cooked quinoa, to serve

1. Heat the oil in a 4-litre/7-pint flameproof casserole. Add the onion, spices, salt and pepper. Fry over a medium-high heat for 5 minutes, until the onion is soft but not coloured.

2. Add the garlic, red pepper and aubergines and fry for a further 5 minutes, until the red pepper and aubergines are beginning to soften.

3. Stir in the chickpeas, tomatoes and stock. Bring to the boil, then reduce the heat and simmer, covered, for 30 minutes.

4. Meanwhile, slice the cabbage leaves into ribbons. Add the cabbage to the casserole, cover and simmer for 10–12 minutes, until the cabbage is tender but still bright green. Taste and adjust the seasoning, adding salt and pepper if using. Serve immediately with cooked quinoa.

VIBRANT CABBAGE

Adding the cabbage towards the end of cooking will help keep its vibrant colour.

PER SERVING: 371 KCALS | 13.5G FAT | 1.9G SAT FAT | 50.9G CARBS | 16.3G SUGARS | 14.5G FIBRE | 12.4G PROTEIN | 1.4G SALT

KALE AND BUTTER BEAN CASSEROLE

Served bubbling hot, this filling casserole of nourishing, nutrient-packed butter beans, onions, tomatoes and kale, finished with a flurry of diced avocado, creates a really wholesome meal, perfect for a chilly winter's day.

SERVES: 6
PREP: 25 MINUTES, PLUS OVERNIGHT SOAKING
COOK: 1¾–2 HOURS

- 350 g/12 oz butter beans, soaked overnight
- 1 tbsp cumin seeds
- 2 tsp dried oregano
- 3 tbsp groundnut oil
- 2 onions, chopped
- 2 garlic cloves, thinly sliced
- 2 fresh red or green chillies, deseeded and sliced
- 400 g/14 oz canned chopped tomatoes
- 450 ml/15 fl oz vegan stock
- 175 g/6 oz shredded kale
- 5 tbsp chopped fresh coriander
- juice of 1 lime
- salt and pepper (optional)
- 2 avocados, cubed and tossed with 1 tsp lime juice, to garnish
- ½ red onion, sliced, to garnish

1. Drain the beans, put them into a large saucepan and cover with water. Bring to the boil, boil for 15 minutes, then simmer for 30–45 minutes, until tender but not disintegrating. Drain and set aside.

2. Put the cumin seeds into a small dry frying pan over a medium heat and fry until fragrant. Add the oregano, fry for a few seconds, then immediately remove the mixture from the pan.

3. Lightly crush the mixture in a mortar with a pestle.

4. Heat the oil in a large, flameproof casserole over a medium heat. Add the chopped onions and the spice and herb mixture. Fry for 5 minutes, until the onions are translucent. Add the garlic and chillies and fry for a further 2 minutes.

5. Stir the tomatoes, beans and stock into the casserole. Season with salt and pepper, if using, and bring to the boil. Reduce the heat, cover and simmer for 30 minutes, stirring occasionally.

6. Increase the heat and stir in the kale. Simmer, uncovered, for 7 minutes, or until tender but still brightly coloured. Stir in the coriander and lime juice.

7. Ladle into soup bowls, garnish with the avocado and red onion and serve immediately.

PER SERVING: 400 KCALS | 15.8G FAT | 2.7G SAT FAT | 52.5G CARBS | 6.9G SUGARS | 14.4G FIBRE | 17.8G PROTEIN | 0.8G SALT

CHICKPEA WALNUT PATTIES

These hearty patties are very similar to falafel, but have the added richness and flavour of walnuts.

SERVES: 4

PREP: 15 MINS, PLUS CHILLING COOK: 10 MINS

2 garlic cloves
1 shallot
425 g/15 oz canned chickpeas, drained and rinsed
15 g/½ oz fresh flat-leaf parsley
1 tsp ground coriander
1 tsp ground cumin
½ tsp salt
⅛ tsp cayenne pepper
2 tbsp olive oil
2 tbsp plain flour
½ tsp baking powder
60 g/2¼ oz roasted, unsalted walnuts, roughly chopped
2 tbsp sunflower oil, for frying

1. Put the garlic and shallot into a food processor and pulse to chop. Add the chickpeas, parsley, coriander, cumin, salt, cayenne pepper, olive oil and flour and pulse to a chunky purée. Add the baking powder and pulse once to incorporate. Add the walnuts and pulse once to incorporate.

2. Shape the chickpea mixture into four equal-sized patties, about 10 cm/4 inches in diameter. Chill in the refrigerator for at least 30 minutes or overnight.

3. Heat the sunflower oil in a large frying pan over a medium-high heat. Add the patties and cook for 4–5 minutes on each side until golden brown. Serve hot.

WHY NOT TRY

Make these delicious patties into the full burger experience by serving on toasted vegan hamburger buns, with a slice of tomato, crunchy lettuce and vegan mayonnaise-style sauce or tahini.

PER SERVING: 320 KCALS | 24.7G FAT | 2.6G SAT FAT | 18.1G CARBS | 3.5G SUGARS | 5.2G FIBRE | 7G PROTEIN | 0.9G SALT

NUT ROAST

This classic vegan dish is always a winner! Serve with tasty fresh vegetables and plenty of vegan gravy.

SERVES: 6
PREP: 20 MINS COOK: 35–40 MINS

1 tbsp olive oil, for brushing
2 tbsp olive oil
1 large onion, finely chopped
100 g/3½ oz ground almonds
100 g/3½ oz cashew nuts, finely chopped
55 g/2 oz fresh wholemeal vegan breadcrumbs
100 ml/3½ fl oz vegan stock
finely grated rind and juice of 1 small lemon
1 tbsp finely chopped fresh rosemary leaves
salt and pepper (optional)
fresh rosemary sprigs and lemon slices, to garnish (optional)

1. Preheat the oven to 200°C/400°F/Gas Mark 6. Brush a 750-ml/1¼-pint loaf tin with oil and line with baking paper.

2. Heat the oil in a large saucepan, add the onion and fry over a medium heat, stirring, for 3–4 minutes until soft.

3. Stir in the almonds, cashew nuts, breadcrumbs, stock, lemon rind and juice and rosemary. Season with salt and pepper, if using, and stir well to mix.

4. Press the mixture into the prepared tin, brush with oil and bake in the preheated oven for 30–35 minutes until golden brown and firm.

5. Turn out and serve hot, garnished with rosemary sprigs, lemon slices and pepper, if using.

IN A NUTSHELL

If you're a vegan, nuts can be an especially important part of your healthy diet as they are a great source of protein and one of the best plant-based sources of healthy fats.

PER SERVING: 289 KCALS | 23.4G FAT | 3G SAT FAT | 16G CARBS | 3.4G SUGARS | 3.3G FIBRE | 7.7G PROTEIN | 0.2G SALT

LEAFY GREENS, LEEK AND ASPARAGUS STIR-FRY

Dark leafy greens are flavoured with ginger, garlic and chilli in this nutrient-packed stir-fry.

SERVES: 6

PREP: 20 MINS COOK: 10 MINS

500 g/1 lb 2 oz mixed leafy greens, such as pak choi, cavolo nero, chard and spinach
225 g/8 oz asparagus
5 tbsp groundnut oil
3-cm/1¼-inch piece fresh ginger, diced
½ fresh green or red chilli, deseeded and diced
3 large garlic cloves, thinly sliced
6 baby leeks, lower green part included, sliced into rounds
3 tbsp vegan stock
2 tbsp soy sauce
½ tsp salt
10 g/¼ oz fresh coriander leaves
1 tsp sesame seeds
1 tbsp toasted sesame oil
pepper (optional)

1. Cut away the stalks and large central ribs from the greens. Slice the stalks into 1-cm/½-inch pieces. Stack the leaves and slice into ribbons.

2. Snap off the woody ends from the asparagus and discard. Chop the stems into 2-cm/¾-inch pieces. Leave the tips whole.

3. Heat a large wok over a high heat and add the groundnut oil. When almost smoking, add the ginger, chilli and garlic. Stir-fry for 30 seconds.

4. Add the leeks, asparagus and the chopped stalks from the greens. Add stock to moisten and stir-fry for a further 2 minutes.

5. Add the sliced leaves, soy sauce, salt and a little pepper, if using, and stir-fry for 3 minutes.

6. Stir in the coriander, sesame seeds and sesame oil and stir-fry for 30 seconds. Serve immediately.

WHY NOT TRY

Try serving this stir-fry with boiled rice or vegan noodles.

PER SERVING: 161 KCALS | 14.2G FAT | 2.3G SAT FAT | 6.8G CARBS | 2.6G SUGARS | 2.9G FIBRE | 3.4G PROTEIN | 1.1G SALT

BEETROOT AND SEED RISOTTO

The beetroot gives this risotto a beautiful jewel-pink colour, which not only makes it taste great but also makes it highly nutritious!

SERVES: 6

PREP: 20 MINS COOK: 1 HOUR

500 g/1 lb 2 oz raw, whole, even-sized beetroot, unpeeled
2 tbsp olive oil
1 onion, finely chopped
1 garlic clove, finely chopped
250 g/9 oz risotto rice
750 ml/1¼ pints vegan stock
200 ml/7 fl oz vegan dry white wine
salt and pepper (optional)

TOPPING

1 tbsp caraway seeds
50 g/1¾ oz fresh white vegan breadcrumbs
½ tsp caster sugar
1 tbsp vegetable oil

1. Place the beetroot in a large saucepan, cover with water and bring to the boil. Cook for 45 minutes, or until the beetroot is soft and can be pierced with a fork. Drain in a colander and peel the beetroot under cold running water – you should be able to slide the skin off. Trim away any stubborn skin with a knife and set aside.

2. Meanwhile, preheat the oven to 180°C/350°F/Gas Mark 4. Heat the oil in a large ovenproof casserole over a medium heat. Fry the onion and garlic for 3–4 minutes, or until translucent. Stir in the rice, stock and 150 ml/5 fl oz of the wine, cover and transfer to the preheated oven. Cook for 30 minutes, until the rice is tender.

3. To make the topping, crush the caraway seeds with a rolling pin and then mix all the topping ingredients together in a small bowl. Transfer to a small frying pan and fry, stirring constantly, over a medium heat for 2–3 minutes. Tip the topping onto a plate to cool.

4. Process approximately a quarter of the beetroot to a smooth purée in a food processor. Chop the remaining beetroot finely. Stir the chopped and puréed beetroot into the risotto along with the remaining wine, and season to taste with salt and pepper, if using. Divide the risotto between six warmed serving plates, sprinkle some of the crumbs on top of each and serve immediately.

PER SERVING: 313 KCALS | 8.3G FAT | 1.4G SAT FAT | 49.3G CARBS | 7.8G SUGARS | 4.5G FIBRE | 5.3G PROTEIN | 1.4G SALT

SMOKY BEAN CHIMICHANGAS

Bring everyone to the table with the smoky and spicy flavours in this tasty and filling chimichanga.

SERVES: 4
PREP: 15-20 MINS COOK: 25-30 MINS

1 tbsp olive oil
2 onions, sliced
1 green pepper, deseeded and sliced
1 red pepper, deseeded and sliced
400 g/14 oz canned black beans, drained and rinsed
2 tsp vegan chipotle chilli paste
3 tbsp vegetable oil
150 g/5½ oz kale, shredded
juice of 1 orange
4 large soft vegan tortillas
salt and pepper (optional)

1. Heat the olive oil in a large frying pan over a medium-low heat. Fry the onions and peppers for 10–12 minutes, or until the onions are translucent but the peppers are still quite firm. Stir in the drained beans and chipotle paste, cook for a further minute, and then remove from the heat.

2. Heat 2 tablespoons of the vegetable oil in a small wok over a high heat. Stir-fry the shredded kale with the orange juice for 4 minutes, or until wilted. Season to taste with salt and pepper, if using.

3. Divide the cooked kale between the tortillas, making a neat pile in the middle of each flatbread. Top the greens with a layer of the bean mixture. Then carefully fold up the sides of the tortillas to make parcels.

4. Heat the remaining vegetable oil in a large frying pan over a medium heat. Fry the chimichanga parcels briefly on both sides (starting with the side where the folds are visible) until crisp and golden. Serve immediately.

SERVING SUGGESTION

These delicious chimichangas taste and look impressive with rice and salad or salsa served on the side.

PER SERVING: 417 KCALS | 17.8G FAT | 2.6G SAT FAT | 50.4G CARBS | 9G SUGARS | 10.7G FIBRE | 12.2G PROTEIN | 0.7G SALT

TAGLIATELLE WITH HAZELNUT PESTO

Fresh and light, this protein-packed main dish is made in a matter of minutes and is totally delicious.

SERVES: 4

PREP: 5 MINS COOK: 10-12 MINS

1 garlic clove, roughly chopped
55 g/2 oz hazelnuts
100 g/3½ oz wild rocket
4 tbsp olive oil
salt and pepper (optional)

HAZELNUT PESTO

1 tsp salt
350 g/12 oz vegan dried tagliatelle
175 g/6 oz fresh or frozen broad beans

1. To make the pesto, place the garlic, hazelnuts, rocket and oil in a food processor and process to a rough paste. Season to taste with salt and pepper, if using.

2. Add 1 teaspoon of the salt to a large pan of water and bring to the boil. Add the pasta, return to the boil and cook for 8–10 minutes, or until tender but still firm to the bite. Add the beans 3–4 minutes before the end of the cooking time.

3. Drain the pasta and beans well, then tip back into the pan. Add the pesto and toss to coat evenly. Serve immediately.

HAIL THE HAZELNUT

These mighty nuts are rich in vitamin E, which can help prevent cataracts and macular degeneration, maintain healthy skin and reduce the risk of dementia.

PER SERVING: 522 KCALS | 22G FAT | 2.5G SAT FAT | 71G CARBS | 3G SUGARS | 9G FIBRE | 15G PROTEIN | 0.1G SALT

DESSERTS AND BAKING

PISTACHIO ICE CREAM

This is a treat you can truly feel good about. Creamy coconut milk and almond milk are sweetened with dates. Earthy pistachio nuts and almond extract give the ice cream an exotic and irresistible flavour.

SERVES: 6
PREP: 10 MINS, PLUS FREEZING COOK: NONE

75 g/2¾ oz shelled unsalted pistachio nuts
350 ml/12 fl oz coconut milk
350 ml/12 fl oz almond milk
9 medjool dates, stoned
1 tsp vanilla extract
½ tsp almond extract

1. You will need an ice-cream maker for this recipe. Put the nuts and about 125 ml/4 fl oz of the coconut milk into a food processor and process to a smooth paste.

2. Put the remaining coconut milk, the almond milk, dates, vanilla extract and almond extract into a blender. Whizz on high speed for 3–5 minutes, until puréed. Add the pistachio paste and process until well combined.

3. Transfer the mixture to the chilled container of an electric ice-cream maker and freeze according to the manufacturer's instructions. The ice cream can be served immediately, or you can transfer it to a freezer-proof container and freeze overnight for a more solid consistency.

POWERFUL PISTACHIOS

These little green gems are high in gamma-tocopherol, a type of vitamin E that may play a role in reducing lung cancer risk. Loaded with potassium and vitamin B6, they can also help keep your nervous system and muscles healthy, boost your mood and bolster your immune system.

PER SERVING: 195 KCALS | 7.5G FAT | 1.8G SAT FAT | 31.6G CARBS | 25.9G SUGARS | 4G FIBRE | 3.5G PROTEIN | 0.1G SALT

LIME AND CHILLI SORBET LOLLIES

These pale, chilli-speckled sorbet sticks are a twist on the classic lemon sorbet, but have a hidden kick from the chilli. For a less spicy version, reduce the amount of chilli.

MAKES: 8
PREP: 15 MINS, PLUS COOLING AND FREEZING
COOK: 10 MINS, PLUS FREEZING

100 g/3½ oz caster sugar
1 red chilli, deseeded and very finely chopped
400 ml/14 fl oz water
4 large limes
8 very thin slices from a small lime

1. Put the sugar, chilli and water in a saucepan. Place over a medium-low heat, stirring, for 6–8 minutes, or until the sugar has dissolved. Increase the heat to medium-high and bring the mixture to the boil, then remove from the heat.

2. Finely grate the rind of two of the limes into the mixture and stir. Cover and allow to cool completely; this will take about 1 hour.

3. Squeeze the juice from the four limes and stir it into the mixture.

4. Pour the mixture into 8 x 60 ml/4 tbsp ice pop moulds and place a lime slice into each mould. Insert the ice-pop sticks and freeze for 5–6 hours, or until firm.

5. To unmould the ice lollies, dip the frozen moulds into warm water for a few seconds and gently release the lollies while holding the sticks.

PER LOLLY: 59 KCALS | TRACE FAT | TRACE SAT FAT | 15.5G CARBS | 13.2G SUGARS | 0.3G FIBRE | 0.2G PROTEIN | TRACE SALT

CHOCOLATE AND AVOCADO PUDDING POTS

Unlike traditional chocolate mousses, this version doesn't need to be chilled and can be served just minutes after making.

MAKES: 4
PREP: 20 MINS COOK: 5 MINS

55 g/2 oz vegan dark chocolate, broken into pieces
1 large ripe avocado, halved and stoned
4 tbsp canned full-fat coconut milk
4 tsp maple syrup
1/2 tsp natural vanilla extract
pinch of sea salt
grated vegan dark chocolate and lightly toasted coconut chips (optional), to decorate

1. Place the chocolate in a heatproof bowl set over a saucepan of gently simmering water and heat for 5 minutes, making sure that the water doesn't touch the base of the bowl.

2. Scoop the avocado flesh from the skin into a food processor. Process until smooth, then add the coconut milk, maple syrup, vanilla extract and salt. Spoon in the melted chocolate and process until smooth.

3. Spoon the mixture into small shot glasses. Decorate the tops with a little grated chocolate and a few toasted coconut chips, if using. Serve immediately or chill in the refrigerator until needed.

HEALTHY FATS

Avocados have a bad press for being high in calories, but they are rich in healthy monounsaturated fat – the good kind that helps maintain healthy cholesterol levels.

PER POT: 246 KCALS | 16.4G FAT | 7.3G SAT FAT | 24.5G CARBS | 16.1G SUGARS | 4.9G FIBRE | 2.4G PROTEIN | 0.4G SALT

COCONUT RICE PUDDING

Coconut milk and soya milk make this vegan rice pudding just as creamy and delicious as the traditional kind made with dairy.

SERVES: 4
PREP: 15-20 MINS COOK: 50-55 MINS

5 cardamom pods
100 g/3½ oz short grain pudding rice
600 ml/1 pint soya milk
400 ml/14 fl oz coconut milk
55 g/2 oz caster sugar
¼ tsp saffron
2 tbsp flaked almonds

1. Crack open the cardamom pods and remove the seeds. Crush the seeds in a pestle and mortar or with a rolling pin. Place the rice, soya milk, coconut milk, sugar, crushed cardamom seeds and saffron in a large saucepan over a low heat. Simmer for 40 minutes, stirring frequently, until the mixture is thick and creamy.

2. Toast the flaked almonds in a dry frying pan over a high heat for 2–3 minutes, or until lightly golden.

3. Serve the rice pudding hot or cold, topped with the toasted almonds.

WHY NOT TRY

Add some chopped banana, grated apple or some fresh berries to this rice pudding for an extra fruit boost.

PER SERVING: 449 KCALS | 26.5G FAT | 19.4G SAT FAT | 46.9G CARBS | 22.3G SUGARS | 2.2G FIBRE | 9.5G PROTEIN | 0.2G SALT

BAKED APPLES

A fruity filling and a sweet red wine glaze give simple baked apples the star treatment in this winter-warming dessert.

SERVES: 4

PREP: 20 MINS COOK: 40-45 MINS

4 cooking apples
1 tbsp lemon juice
50 g/1¾ oz blueberries
50 g/1¾ oz raisins
25 g/1 oz mixed nuts, toasted and chopped
½ tsp ground cinnamon
2 tbsp soft brown sugar
275 ml/9 oz vegan red wine
2 tsp cornflour
4 tsp water

1. Preheat the oven to 200°C/400°F/Gas Mark 6. Using a sharp knife, score a line around the centre of each apple. Core the apples, then brush the centres with the lemon juice to prevent discoloration. Transfer them to a small roasting tin.

2. Put the blueberries and raisins into a bowl, then add the nuts, cinnamon and sugar. Mix together well. Pile the mixture into the centres of the apples, then pour over the wine.

3. Transfer the stuffed apples to the preheated oven and bake for 40–45 minutes, or until tender. Remove from the oven, then lift the apples out of the roasting tin, set aside and keep warm.

4. Blend the cornflour with the water, then add the mixture to the cooking juices in the roasting tin. Transfer to the hob and cook over a medium heat, stirring, until thickened. Remove from the heat and pour over the apples. Serve.

WHY NOT TRY

Bake the apples in elderflower wine or diluted elderflower cordial instead of red wine.

PER SERVING: 287 KCALS | 4.4G FAT | 0.3G SAT FAT | 52.1G CARBS | 37.7G SUGARS | 6.5G FIBRE | 2.2G PROTEIN | TRACE SALT

ZESTY LIME PIE

This delicious tart features a crisp base made with coconut oil and a zesty lime filling.

SERVES: 8

PREP: 25 MINS, PLUS CHILLING COOK: 12-15 MINS

BASE

100 g/3½ oz coconut oil
270 g/9½ oz wholemeal plain flour
8 tbsp cold water
1 tbsp wholemeal plain flour, for dusting

FILLING

570 g/1 lb 4½ oz firm tofu
60 ml/2 fl oz lime juice
175 g/6 oz brown sugar
1 tbsp cornflour
2 tsp lime zest

1. Preheat the oven to 200°C/400°F/Gas Mark 6.

2. To make the base, rub the coconut oil into the flour and gradually add the water to bring the dough together. This can be done by hand or using a food processor.

3. Roll out the dough on a work surface lightly dusted with flour and use to line a 25-cm/10-inch loose-based tart tin. Bake in the preheated oven for 12–15 minutes, until golden and crisp. Leave to cool.

4. Place all the ingredients for the filling except the lime zest in the bowl of a food processor and process for 1–2 minutes, until smooth. Stir in the lime zest.

5. Spoon the tart filling into the pastry case, smoothing it with a rubber spatula. Chill in the refrigerator for at least 1 hour before serving.

WHY NOT TRY

Try decorating the tart with grated vegan chocolate, a sprinkle of desiccated coconut or slices of fresh lime.

PER SERVING: 424 KCALS | 19.7G FAT | 11.9G SAT FAT | 52.2G CARBS | 21.6G SUGARS | 5.6G FIBRE | 16.1G PROTEIN | TRACE SALT

CHOCOLATE CAKE WITH AVOCADO ICING

This deliciously rich vegan chocolate cake is topped with a smooth icing that has an unusual secret ingredient!

SERVES: 8
PREP: 25 MINS, PLUS COOLING AND CHILLING
COOK: 30-35 MINS

1 tbsp vegetable oil, for oiling
250 g/9 oz self-raising wholemeal flour
50 g/1¾ oz vegan cocoa powder
250 g/9 oz demerara sugar
1 tsp bicarbonate of soda
1 tsp instant coffee powder
75 g/2¾ oz coconut oil
250 ml/8 ½ fl oz almond milk
1 tsp vanilla extract
1 tsp vegan apple cider vinegar

ICING
2 ripe avocados
40 g/1½ oz vegan cocoa powder
1½ tbsp vegan icing sugar
4 tbsp agave nectar
½ tsp vanilla extract

1. Preheat the oven to 180°C/350°F/Gas Mark 4. Oil a 20-cm/8-inch round cake tin and line with baking paper.

2. Sift the flour and cocoa into a mixing bowl. Stir in the sugar, bicarbonate of soda and coffee powder.

3. Melt the coconut oil in the microwave or in a small saucepan. Transfer to a heatproof jug and stir in the almond milk, vanilla extract and vinegar.

4. Pour the liquid ingredients onto the dry ingredients in the mixing bowl, beat together thoroughly and spoon into the prepared tin. Smooth the top with a rubber spatula.

5. Bake in the preheated oven for 30–35 minutes. Leave to cool in the tin for 10 minutes, then turn out onto a wire rack and leave to cool completely.

6. To make the icing, peel and stone the avocados. Mash the flesh and pass through a sieve. Transfer to a small mixing bowl, add the remaining ingredients and beat together thoroughly. Chill in the refrigerator for 20 minutes, then spread evenly over the top of the cake.

COOK'S TIP

Passing the avocado through a sieve will prevent green flecks appearing in your icing. Ripe avocados will make this easier.

PER SERVING: 465 KCALS | 21.1G FAT | 10.4G SAT FAT | 71.9G CARBS | 38.5G SUGARS | 11G FIBRE | 7.5G PROTEIN | 0.4G SALT

CARROT CAKE

This variation on a familiar favourite cake is sweetened with fruit. It is also packed with delicious nuts and has an icing made from almonds.

SERVES: 8
PREP: 20 MINS, PLUS COOLING AND CHILLING
COOK: 40-45 MINS

1 tbsp vegetable oil, for oiling
200 g/7 oz dates
150 g/5½ oz sultanas
250 ml/8½ fl oz boiling water
100 g/3½ oz walnuts
100 g/3½ oz carrots, grated
300 g/10½ oz plain wholemeal flour
1 tsp ground cinnamon
1 tsp baking powder
1 tsp bicarbonate of soda
125 ml/4 fl oz apple juice

ICING

100 g/3½ oz cashew nuts
3 tbsp maple syrup
1 tsp vanilla extract
1 tsp ground cinnamon
zest of 1 lemon

1. Preheat the oven to 180°C/350°F/Gas Mark 4. Oil and line an 18-cm/7-inch round loose-based cake tin.

2. Stone and roughly chop the dates. Place them in a small bowl with the sultanas and add the boiling water. Set the ingredients aside to soak.

3. Roughly chop the walnuts and place in a large mixing bowl with the grated carrot. Add the flour, cinnamon, baking powder and bicarbonate of soda and mix thoroughly.

4. Add the dates and sultanas with the soaking water and the apple juice. Mix thoroughly. Spoon into the prepared tin and smooth the top with a rubber spatula.

5. Bake in the centre of the preheated oven for 40–45 minutes, until cooked through. Leave to cool in the tin for 10 minutes, then turn out onto a wire rack and leave to cool completely.

6. To make the icing, soak the nuts in boiling water for 30 minutes, then drain. Put the nuts, maple syrup, vanilla extract and cinnamon into a blender and process until smooth. Stir in the lemon zest and chill in the refrigerator for 20 minutes before spreading evenly over the top of the cake.

WHY NOT TRY

Try using orange juice or carrot juice in place of the apple juice.

PER SERVING: 448 KCALS | 16.4G FAT | 2G SAT FAT | 73.3G CARBS | 34.1G SUGARS | 8.5G FIBRE | 10.4G PROTEIN | 0.6G SALT

SUPERFOOD CHOCOLATE BARK

Turn vegan chocolate into an extra special and nutritious treat by studding it with delicious nuts, berries and seeds.

SERVES: 6
PREP: 20 MINS, PLUS SETTING
COOK: 5 MINS

100 g/3½ oz vegan chocolate with 85% cocoa, broken into pieces
25 g/1 oz Brazil nuts, roughly chopped
25 g/1 oz unblanched almonds, roughly chopped
25 g/1 oz pistachio nuts, roughly chopped
2 tbsp dried goji berries, roughly chopped
2 tbsp dried cranberries, roughly chopped
1 tbsp chia seeds

1. Place the chocolate in a heatproof bowl set over a saucepan of gently simmering water and heat for 5 minutes until melted.

2. Line a large baking sheet with non-stick baking paper. Stir the chocolate, then pour it onto the paper and quickly spread it out to a 20 x 30-cm/8 x 12-inch rectangle.

3. Sprinkle the Brazil nuts, almonds, pistachio nuts, goji berries, cranberries and chia seeds over the top, then leave to set in a cool place.

4. To serve, lift the chocolate off the paper and break into rough-shaped shards. Store in a plastic container in the refrigerator for up to 3 days.

POWERFUL CHOCOLATE

Generally speaking, the more cocoa solids that chocolate contains, the more antioxidants and minerals it has.

PER SERVING: 227 KCALS | 15.7G FAT | 5.3G SAT FAT | 17.79G CARBS | 10.2G SUGARS | 5.1G FIBRE | 5.1G PROTEIN | TRACE SALT

FIG AND OAT BITES

The goodness of wholegrain oats paired with fibre-rich dried figs creates these scrumptious nuggets of goodness that contain no added sugar or salt. A sprinkling of chia seeds and spices boosts their feel-good factor further.

MAKES: 25
PREP: 20–25 MINS, PLUS COOLING COOK: 20 MINS

450 g/1 lb soft dried figs
3 tbsp coconut oil, at room temperature
½ tsp ground ginger
½ tsp ground cinnamon
juice of 1 large orange
200 g/7 oz rolled oats
1 tbsp chia seeds

1. Preheat the oven to 180° C/350° F/Gas Mark 4. Line a 23-cm/9-inch square baking tin with baking paper.

2. Place the dried figs, coconut oil, ginger and cinnamon into a food processor and pulse until roughly chopped. Add the orange juice and oats and pulse again until the mixture just comes together. If a little dry, add a touch more orange juice; if a little wet, stir through a few more oats. Add the chia seeds and pulse again very briefly.

3. Spoon the mixture into the prepared baking tin. Use the back of a greased spatula to push the mixture to the corners and spread it evenly.

4. Bake in the preheated oven for 20 minutes. Remove from the oven and, using a sharp knife, cut into 25 small squares. Leave to cool completely on a wire rack and then serve.

FABULOUS FIGS

Originating in Asia, figs have an illustrious history. They are high in natural sugars, which, like dates, make them perfect for adding a healthier dose of sweetness to any dish.

PER SQUARE: 93 KCALS | 2.4G FAT | 1.5G SAT FAT | 17.5G CARBS | 9G SUGARS | 2.8G FIBRE | 1.7G PROTEIN | TRACE SALT

COCONUT, CACAO AND HAZELNUT TRUFFLES

This super-charged and tasty power snack is crammed with natural ingredients, creating the perfect energy-giving pick-me-up.

MAKES: 20
PREP: 25 MINS, PLUS STORING COOK: NONE

85 g/3 oz unblanched hazelnuts
55 g/2 oz cacao nibs
6 soft dried figs, roughly chopped
25 g/1 oz desiccated coconut
1 tbsp maple syrup
finely grated zest and juice of 1/2 small orange
1 tbsp finely chopped cacao nibs, for coating
2 tbsp desiccated coconut, for coating

1. Add the hazelnuts and the cacao nibs to a food processor and process until everything is very finely chopped.

2. Add the figs, coconut, maple syrup and orange zest and juice to the processor, and process until finely chopped and the mixture has come together in a ball.

3. Scoop the mixture out of the food processor, then cut into 20 even-sized pieces. Roll into small balls in your hands.

4. Mix the chopped cacao nibs with the coconut on a sheet of non-stick baking paper or a plate. Roll the truffles, one at a time, in the cacao and coconut mixture, then arrange in a small plastic container. Store in the refrigerator for up to 3 days.

RAW CACAO

Unlike cocoa powder, which is made by roasting cacao at high temperatures, raw cacao is cold-pressed to retain more minerals and antioxidants.

PER TRUFFLE: 46 KCALS | 3.5G FAT | 1G SAT FAT | 3.2G CARBS | 2.1G SUGARS | 0.9G FIBRE | 1.3G PROTEIN | TRACE SALT

SWEET POTATO AND PECAN FILO PARCELS

You might not expect a savoury filling in a sweet treat but these delicious crisp filo parcels are filled with a spicy mix of silky sweet potato and crunchy pecan nuts.

MAKES: 12

PREP: 15 MINS, PLUS COOLING COOK: 10–12 MINS

1 large sweet potato (about 280 g/10 oz), baked, peeled and mashed
60 g/2¼ oz shelled pecan nuts, finely chopped
⅛ tsp freshly ground nutmeg
1½ tsp very finely chopped fresh ginger
4 tsp coconut sugar
1 tsp lemon juice
4 x 44 x 24-cm/17½ x 9½-inch vegan filo pastry sheets
1 tbsp hazelnut or olive oil, for brushing
10 g/¼ oz vegan icing sugar mixed with ½ tsp ground cinnamon, for dusting

1. Preheat the oven to 200°C/400°F/Gas Mark 6. Line a baking tray with a silicone sheet.

2. Mix the sweet potato and half the nuts together in a bowl. Add the nutmeg, ginger, sugar and lemon juice, mixing well with a fork.

3. Unroll the sheets of filo pastry and stack on a board with the long edge facing you. Using a ruler or metal edge as a guide, slice crossways into three 44 x 8-cm/17 x 3¼-inch strips. Work with one strip at a time, covering the remaining strips with a clean damp tea towel to prevent them drying out.

4. Lightly brush the upper surface of one filo strip with oil. Lightly sprinkle with a few of the remaining nuts.

5. Place a tablespoon of the sweet potato mixture in the bottom left-hand corner of the pastry strip and lightly mould it into a rough triangle. Fold the pastry over diagonally to form a triangle. Continue to fold in triangles until you reach the end of the strip.

6. Brush both sides of the parcel with oil and place on the baking tray. Repeat with the remaining 11 filo strips.

7. Bake in the preheated oven for 10–12 minutes, turning halfway through the cooking time, or until golden and crisp.

8. Transfer to a wire rack and leave to cool slightly. Lightly dust all over with the icing sugar and cinnamon mixture. Serve immediately.

SWEET ENOUGH

Coconut sugar is used as a sweetener – it has an intense flavour so go steady as you will need only a small amount.

PER PARCEL: 114 KCALS | 5.1G FAT | 0.5G SAT FAT | 15.7G CARBS | 3.7G SUGARS | 1.6G FIBRE | 1.9G PROTEIN | 0.1G SALT

INDEX